Phonics for Pre K

Children's Reading & Writing Education Books

All Rights reserved. No part of this book may be reproduced or used in any way or form or by any means whether electronic or mechanical, this means that you cannot record or photocopy any material ideas or tips that are provided in this book.

Copyright 2016

Learning Basic Phonics

Ant

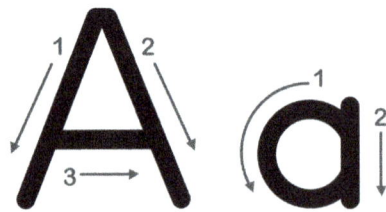

Butterfly

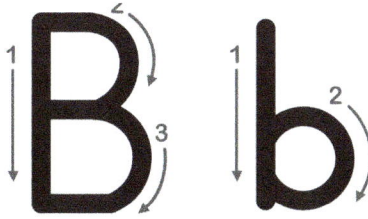

Cat

C c

Dog

D d

Elephant

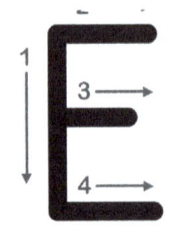 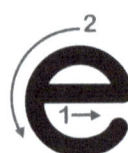 

Frog

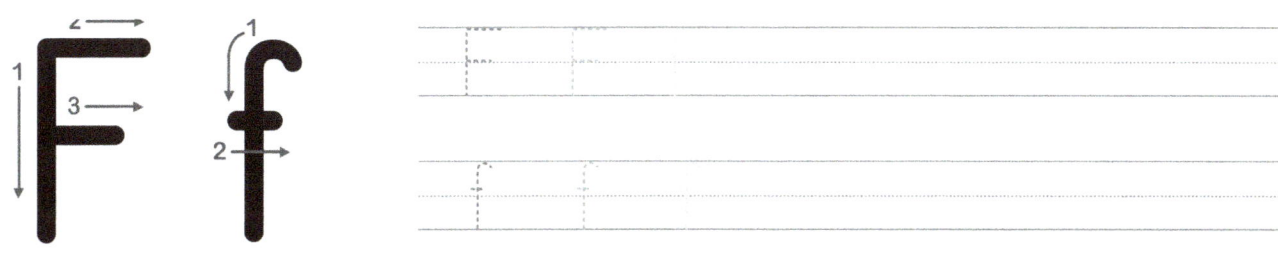

Giraffe

Hippopotamus

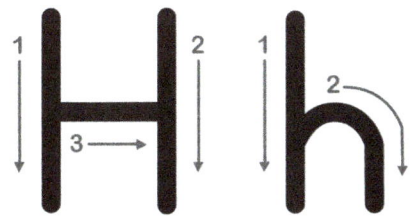

Iguana

Jellyfish

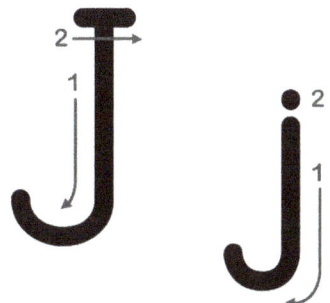

Kangaroo

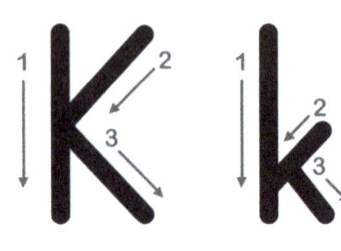

Lion

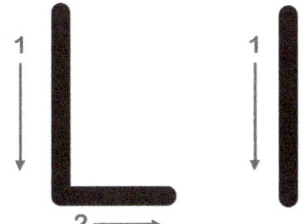

Monkey

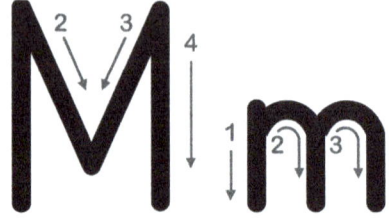

M m

Needlefish

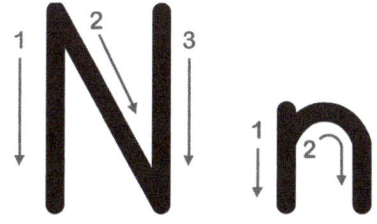

Owl

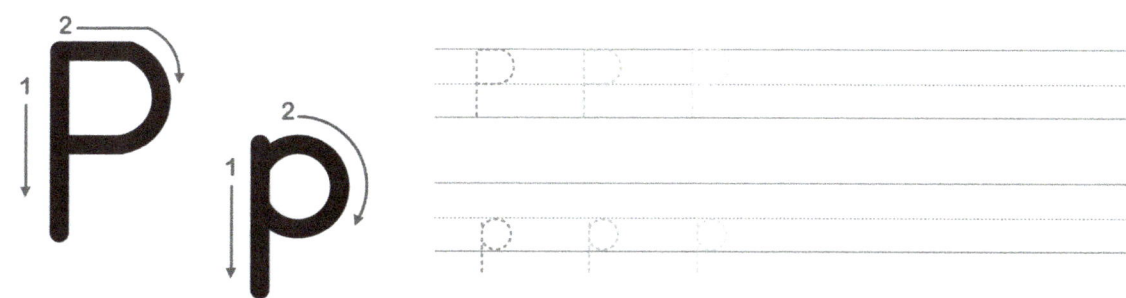

Panda

Quail

Rabbit

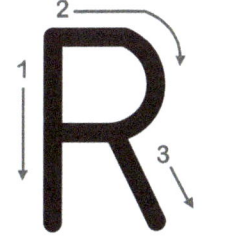 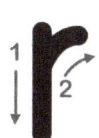

Sheep

S s

Turtle

T t

Unicorn

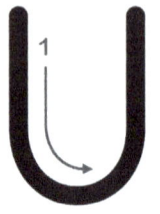 

Viper

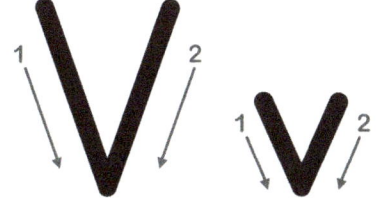

Worm

W w

X-ray Fish

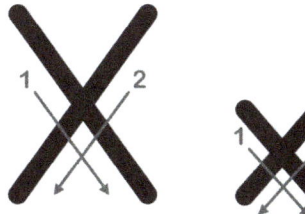

Yak

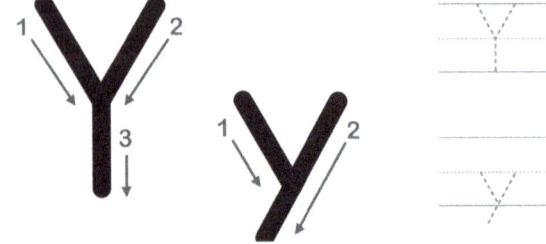

Zebra

Z z

Practice Writing

Trace and rewrite the following words

Aa - Cc

Art Art

Bed Bed

Cup Cup

Ee - Gg

Eat Eat

Fit Fit

Get Get

Hh - Kk

Hot Hot

Jet Jet

Kit Kit

Ll - Nn

Lip   Lip

Met   Met

Nod   Nod

Oo - Qq

Ode Ode

Pet Pet

Quo Quo

Rr - Ss

Rat Rat

Set Set

Top Top

Uu - Ww

Up Up

Via Via

Wet Wet

Ss - Zz

Six Six

Yes Yes

Zoo Zoo

Awesome!

Good Job! Keep up the Good Work!

www.ingramcontent.com/pod-product-compliance
Lightning Source LLC
LaVergne TN
LVHW082254070426
835507LV00037B/2287